CW00469814

A HA]
BRAIN

Switch On Your Brain. Boost Your
Serotonin, Dopamine, Oxytocin, &
Endorphin Levels. Unlock Your
Happier, Healthier & More Abundant
Life

ABUZAR KHAN

Copyright © 2023 by Abuzar Khan All rights reserved.

No part of this book may be reproduced in any form without permission in writing from the author. No part of this publication may be reproduced or transmitted in any form or by any means, mechanical or electronic, including photocopying or recording, or by any information storage and retrieval system, or transmitted by email or by any other means whatsoever without permission in writing from the author.

DEDICATION

**Dedicated To Every Single Reader
Who Is Eager To Discover The Hidden
Power of His Brain And Is Ready To
Explore The Neuroscience of
Happiness And Success.**

Neuroscience is by far the most exciting branch of science because the brain is the most fascinating object in the universe. Every human brain is different - the brain makes each human unique and defines who he or she is.

Stanley B. Prusiner

Table of Contents

Introduction

She was crying continuously during the session and was saying that I had stabbed my soul upon him, why did this happen to my love? She started telling. Do you know? In the beginning of love, both of us did not care about anything other than each other for nine or ten days. We were neither conscious of food nor of sleep. We were madly in love. That's when we realized we were meant for each other. We have a spiritual relationship.

She started crying again. He offered her tissue and water and asked what happened then? She said, after ten days, we slowly drifted away from each other. He started to hate my laugh which he liked very much, my face which he used to see standing in the street light for hours, now months have passed he has never seen my face. This love of ours started after marriage, but after ten days, someone might have done black magic. I am very worried.

He saw then and said that the love that you are thinking of soul connection and birth is actually the perfection of dopamine and its companion hormones.

After starting a new romantic relationship, the levels of dopamine and its accompanying hormones are so high that the time spent under its influence seems wonderful. You see the good even in the evil of your partner, hunger and sleep fly away and every thought belongs to him. But as soon as the hormone levels are normal, the love fades away and the partner's snoring and laughter start to fade away. People in the West have understood this concept, so they don't rush to make decisions and let the hormones take their toll. But in the sub-continent, we tend to make relationships difficult, but Indian films make up for it. Each person is a self-confident and stubborn lover like a hero.

You are a very bad doctor. Today is my last session with you. Do you know what love is? I am well aware of my love. I know myself very well. She made a face and left trapped in the vortex of her stubbornness.

The human brain is the center of all philosophical and psychological approaches from the beginning of the world. Most philosophers and researchers had spent a large amount of their life to know the working style of the human brain and how it generates human happiness, success, and blissful life.

It is a daily routine that we experience two types of people who live on the earth. One who wins and the other one fails. One who floats in the ocean of happiness, while the other's life is full of miseries and sadness. One who is confident in all his time and the second one is disappointed with all he posses. One who searches for happiness in his inner world and the second one who seeks happiness in the outer world, the one who remains positive in all types of situations, and the second one who remains unhappy in all positive situations and gets failure. Then, what is the difference between them?

The basic difference lies in the knowledge of usage of the human brain, and its working style. We can say that the brain is the primary organ of the human body which creates all kinds of happiness, success, and misery. In other words, that the brain is the source of all the qualities that define our humanity.

For centuries, scientists and philosophers have been fascinated by the brain, and they have made unaccountable efforts to know the secrets of the brain but now, however, they have succeeded in their research as the brain is beginning to open its secrets. Scientists have learned more about the brain in the last few years than in all previous centuries because of the accelerating pace of research in neurological and behavioral sciences and by the development of new research and techniques we can understand about brain more and more.

In 1990, the invention of *fMRI* was the game-changer in the field of neuroscience, as it enabled man to observe the activity of the human brain's working process and to know its working style during a special condition like meditation and thinking.

During the Covid–19 pandemic, people from all walks of life were living in fear, anxiety, and depression; this book would try to present some proven technical support to rewire your brain to achieve unconditional happiness using your happy chemicals generated by the paradigm shift in the thinking.

Here, we will focus to understand the neuroscience of happiness, the mental process of the human brain, how the human brain works and how does it affect human life.

What do you expect from this book?

The main objective of this book is to provide you the scientific information on how to build a happier brain. It is my humble effort to help you work towards an elusive state of the brain known as Happiness. First, we'll go through the happiness pursuit, why we need a happier brain, and how to achieve alpha state of brain, and then we will discuss happy chemicals and their vast relation with human happiness, as well as how tiny changes in the thinking process can generate a vast range of happiness.

Hope you will enjoy reading this book and are ready to trigger your happy chemicals to be happy in all spheres of life.

Chapter 1

The Pursuit of Happiness

Happiness is not something ready-made. It comes from your own actions

Dalai Lama XIV

The pursuit of happiness has been an eternal pursuit for mankind. All human actions are directed towards the attainment of a state of happiness. But before we move on to this topic, we should ask two questions that need to be answered. One, what is happiness and the other, what gives happiness. It may be that both the questions are related, but without their answer it would be pointless to talk about happiness.

Coming to the first question 'what is happiness', we first need to understand that creation itself is a puzzle. For an infant, the satisfaction of basic needs leads to a pleasurable experience. For a mother, seeing a baby happy can bring joy, with growth and maturity, the concept of happiness changes. It is no longer about the satisfaction of one, two or three needs. It is about a series of needs that keep arising one after the other.

And this fact answers the second question 'what gives happiness'.

But there is another very intriguing aspect. Happiness is not an innate drive. Rather, it is a conditioned response that is learned through the principle of daily practice. Thus, there can be individual, cultural and societal differences in both the definition and perception of happiness. Psychologists have also given many interpretations of the term "Happiness" but there is a general agreement about hedonic experience or the pleasure principle.

Happiness has different meanings in western values, while the Indian interpretation is altogether different. So it is Ananda that is the determinant of happiness from the Western point of view, while the Indian point of view talks about Ananda or Bliss, which is a spiritual mental state.

Naturally, in the Western approach of happiness would be determined more by physical and material experiences, whereas in the Indian ethos "Santosh" or inner feeling would determine it. Happiness is a derived state where many factors play a role, the most important being behavioral disposition. Thus the root of happiness lies in the way a person interprets experiences, both sensory as well as mental.

Aristotle came to the conclusion that what man wants above all is to be happy.

Not only do we seek happiness for its own sake, but all other pursuits—health, beauty, honor, money, or power—have value only because we expect them to make us happy. "Life, liberty, and the pursuit of happiness" are the inalienable rights of a person.

So, what is happiness? This is a vague concept.

Modern science defines happiness as the positive range of emotions we feel when we are satisfied or filled with joy.

Not very clear, is it? A quote from Charles Spurgeon may provide a better definition of happiness.

"It's not how much we have, but how much we enjoy that makes us happy."

Lyubomirsky defines a happy person as one who frequently experiences positive emotions, such as happiness, interest, and pride, and infrequently experiences negative emotions, such as sadness, anxiety, and anger. Actually happiness is an individual's approach; it has different meaning for different people.

Osho narrates a story to emphasize this......

Four women sat under hair dryers in a beauty parlor for hours. After finishing their gossip, they turned to philosophy. "Happiness is when my husband brings home his paycheck," the first lady said.

"Happiness is gambling in Las Vegas and winning," said another woman.

A third woman commented, "Happiness is vacationing without my husband or my kids."

"Happiness is eating without worrying about calories," concluded a fourth woman.

After listening, one hairdresser whispered to another, "Happiness is not listening to these cackling hens."

It is clear that there is no universal definition of the idea of happiness - it is a personal phenomenon.

But although there are many different definitions of happiness; It is often described as involving positive emotions and life satisfaction. But real happiness is an emotional state that develops from feelings of happiness, contentment, and fulfillment.

When most people talk about happiness, they may be talking about how they are feeling in the present moment, or they may be talking about a more common sense of how they feel about life as a whole.

Happiness is a broadly defined term. Psychologists and other social scientists commonly use the term 'subjective well-being' when talking about this elusive emotional state. As it sounds, subjective well-being currently focuses on a person's overall personal feelings about their life.

In the book, Power Up Your Brain, The Neuroscience of Enlightenment, David, Perlmutter, M.D., FACN. Alberto Villodo, Ph.D. Say "*If we take the Eastern attributes of the Enlightenment out of their religious context and place them within the realm of biological science, we find that they are properties associated with activation of the prefrontal cortex—the newest part of the human brain. On functional MRI scans, people who meditate regularly have developed brains that are wired differently than the brains of people who don't meditate. They are able to stay calm and relaxed, live at peaceful state, and practice compassion. Curiously, his prefrontal cortex is the most active area in his brain during states he describes as samadhi or enlightenment".*

The philosophy of happiness has deep rooted in ancient Greek phenomena, where we find two philosophers who have different perspectives on the philosophy of Happiness.

According to the philosopher Aristippus (435–256 BC) happiness is just a pleasure, while the values have no real worth to him. Aristippus thinking approach inspired the term "hedonic pleasure" a label often given to the temporary relief of impulsive and indulgent pleasures or urges.

In contrast "eudemonic happiness" taught by Aristotle (384–322 BCE) derives from deep well-being in aligning with purpose, overcoming obstacles and achieving growth and real-life success.

This happiness has grown from a virtuous life and the pursuit of realizing our potential. Aristippus and Aristotle may have been there before the beginning of cognitive neuroscience but their thinking pointed put to something we now know to be true.

Hedonic Pleasure

Hedonic happiness is a matter of momentum. Pleasure comes from doing things that give a sense of pleasure like a good meal and sexual intimacy and what provides you pleasure for a while. It is often associated with doing what feels good, self-care, fulfilling desires, experiencing joy, and feeling a sense of satisfaction.

Different feelings of happiness are related to the presence of different brain chemicals. Hedonic pleasures are, in general, the domain of dopamine: the chemical often associated with the pursuit of the desired object. Getting urges, being distracted, or "just one more" is usually dopamine-spiked behavior that doesn't usually lead to lasting gratification.

Eudaimonic Happiness

Eudaimonic Happiness comes from virtue and the search for the meaning of life. There are some important components of eudemonic well-being, which include feeling that one's life has meaning, value and purpose. It is more associated with fulfilling responsibilities, investing in long-term goals, concern for the welfare of other people, and living up to personal ideals. Eudemonic rewards, on the other hand, are associated with a different chemical: serotonin, which increases feelings of worthiness, belonging, and self-esteem. Dopamine and serotonin both help you feel pleasure and happiness.

Hedonic and eudemonia are referred to as pleasure and meaning in psychology today respectively. Recently psychologists have suggested adding a third component related to engagement. These are feelings of commitment and participation in different areas of life.

All of these can play an important role in the overall experience of happiness, although the relative value of each can be highly subjective. Some activities can be both enjoyable and meaningful, while others can be skewed in some way or the other.

Different Feeling of Happiness

- **Bliss:** a brief feeling that is felt in the present moment
- **Excitement**: a pleasant feeling that involves looking forward to something with positive anticipation
- **Gratitude**: a positive emotion that includes being grateful and appreciated
- **Pride**: a sense of satisfaction in what you have achieved
- **Optimism**: a way of looking at life from a positive, enthusiastic perspective
- **Contentment**: This type of happiness involves a feeling of satisfaction.

How Do You Know That You Are Happy?

While the perception of happiness can vary from person to person, there are some important cues that psychologists look for when measuring and assessing happiness.

Key signs of happiness

• Feeling like you're living the life you've wanted

• Feeling that your living conditions are good

•Feeling that you have accomplished (or will accomplish) what you want in life

• Feeling satisfied with your life

• Feeling more positive than negative

An important thing to remember is that happiness is the overall feeling of experiencing more positive emotions than negative ones.

The pursuit of happiness has two major components:

•**Balance of emotions**: Everyone experiences feelings, emotions, and moods, both positive and negative. Happiness is usually associated with experiencing more positive emotions than negative ones.

• **Life satisfaction**: This refers to how satisfied you feel with different areas of your life, including your relationships, work, achievements, and other things that you consider important.

- Feeling good all the time.

- Being rich and being able to afford everything you want.

- Being the most powerful person on earth.

- Even if everything in your life isn't perfect.

The important thing to understand is that happiness is both a relative as well as an absolute construct. And it's the tricky aspect of happiness that makes it complicated. Nevertheless, the pursuit of happiness is a continuous pursuit of man. The search for an elusive formula for happiness is a persistent aspect of human psychology. Thus, although there is no definite answer as to what happiness is and what gives happiness, trial and error processes go on.

So, one idea suggests that according to the World Happiness Report 2016 it is money that gives happiness, whatever the truth, the fact remains that happiness is a desired state. How this can be achieved can have innumerable answers, ranging from one extreme where it is the satisfaction of endless desires that keep arising one after another to the other extreme where it is the end of desire.

Either way, it is the person whose mindset will determine what happiness is and what it gives. However, the all-important conclusion is that happiness is a momentary experience and that the pursuit of eternal happiness may be a short-lived desire. The best solution is to stop looking for a formula and try to control the brain chemicals which are the root cause of all happiness and unhappiness. Research won't help. One has to search within.

Osho states, "Happiness is not the result. It is a way of life. It's an attitude, not a desire. "You can be happy here and now if you know how to be, but you'll never be happy if you don't know how to be and you keep wishing for it. Happiness is an art. It's life. There is a way."

However we look at it, happiness can only be built on the foundation of a calm, stable brain. This is the simple secret of happiness. If we want to be happy, we should enjoy what we are doing and not let the past or the future occupy our brain. We must stay firmly in the present and try to find the beauty of life at every step.

Chapter 2

Why You Need A Happier Brain

"Happiness is not a readymade thing. It comes from your own tasks. ~ Dalai Lama

Today's hectic world a happier brain is the need of hours for the overall well being of any one. If one is able to build a happier brain, his overall life becomes more pleasant and clear. There are huge benefits of having happy brain in many areas of life, whether they are personal, professional, relationship etc. by understanding the psychology and neuroscience of happiness and we can implement some powerful habits to happen miracles, this book is all set to focus on happiness psychology and neuroscience to provide details of how one can become happy.

We all know that happiness is the only thing humans needs. All kind of inventions of the world is the result of seeking comfort and making human lives easier.

Happiness is nothing but an emotional state of pleasantness, just like any other feelings of fear, anger, love etc. the ultimate desire of any man to be in a constant state of happiness, and this desire is strong the time he/she is born on this planet. Nobody ever wants to go through pain, and everyone wants to get as many feelings of pleasure as possible.

Tony Robbins, world renowned motivational speaker and performer strategist, says that all our behavior and actions are influenced by two reasons, either to avoid pain or to increase pleasure. Whatever you do in your life, the main motivation behind that activity cannot be anything else except reducing your pain or increasing your level of Happiness. All inventions like airplanes, smart phones, or televisions, were created to improve our comfort level or provide us with a more enjoyable life experience.

The essential point here is that we only take action to invite more people happiness in our life. The quality or direction of our actions can be is flawed, and we may need some guidance, but it is within us to find happiness. Happiness is definitely a choice. It depends on the action or behavior we choose in our lives.

In fact, if we are happy, we can generate innumerable positivity in all areas of our live. When we are happy, we not only feel more joy, satisfaction, love, pride, and amazement, but at the same time, we also improve in other aspects of our lives: our energy levels, our immune system, our engagement with and at work other people, and our physical and mental health. We also strengthen a sense of self-confidence and self-esteem; we believe that we develop self-compassion, and feel worthy of respect. When we become successful in making happier brain, we not only improve the quality of our lives, but we also share the benefits of our happiness with our partners, families, communities, and even society at large.

You need happier brain because Happier Brain stimulates the development of neurological contacts and improves cognition by increasing mental productivity. Happier brain improves your ability to analyze and think and affects the vision around you.

This is a quick list of the different types of benefits that resulted of having happier brain.

- Improves heart rate
- Copes with stress more effectively
- Builds a strong immune system
- Creates an overall healthy lifestyle
- Reduces pain
- Increases longevity of life
- Leads to better decision making and problem solving
- Improves individual and team productivity

- Helps you be more productive, consequently earning more.

Chapter 3

Train Your Brain To Be Happier

"The brain is like a muscle. When it is in use we feel very good. Understanding is joyous". Carl Sagan

If you want to be happy in every situation for the rest of your life, make sure your brain would generate happy hormones .Why? Because being happy is more important to your brain as much as you can. But how can we get into that very particular state of happiness. The answer is very simple that we have to train our brain to think positively and kill all negative patterns attacking upon us time to time. Our brain has been designed to think negatively which make us feel stressed and unhappy, although we have lots of positive things to be happy. So we are in dire need to train our brain to kill everything that has negative impact upon us and focus on generating happiness.

One of the oldest principles of neuroscience has been that our mental process begins with mental activity: that when it comes to the creation and formation of our brain, our brain is in charge. However, recent research has shown that it can work in another way: it focuses; repeated mental activity can affect your brain structure, wiring and changes in abilities.

We can literally shrink different areas of the brain, fire circuits or tamper with them. The more you ask your brain to do, the more cartilage sets to handle new tasks. It responds by making a strong connection to the circuits that understands the desired behavior or thinking and weakens contacts with others. That way, what you do and what you think, see or feel is in line with your brain connections to meet the size of your brain and your needs.

What does all this mean? This means that what we think, and what we say is important. That it affects who we become outside inside and in the brain. Mostly, this means that you can train your brain to be more positive.

Start thinking of pleasant thoughts, look at the bright aspects, and focus on your brain again when negative thoughts come. You have the ability to determine how your brain thinks about events in your life. Use it for your benefit to reset the events and think positively.

Your thoughts make your role, how you work in the world, and how much you travel mentally, physically and spiritually. You are what you think you are, and all your actions go beyond thinking. Your internal thoughts will always appear in your external conditions as the changes that make up your life always occur before changes in your thinking style.

As far as your brain is concerned, every thought releases brain chemicals. By focusing on negative thoughts, the brain effectively eliminates its positive strength, slows down, and can dim your brain's ability to work, even produces depression.

On the other hand, positive thinking, happy, optimistic, hopeful, cheerful ideas reduce cortisol and produce serotonin, which creates a sense of fitness. This helps your brain work on top capacity.

Pleasant thoughts and positive thinking, in general, helps and strengthens new synapses, as well as in your prefrontal cortex (PFC) which is the center of integration of all the functions of your brain. In other words, your PFC not only controls the signals that move your neurons to other parts of the brain and your body, but also thinking about what you are physically doing to and this allows to consider.

In particular, the PFC allows you to control your emotional response through a connection to your deep -long brain. It gives you the ability to focus on whatever choice you make and to gain insight into your thinking process.

PFC is the only part of your brain that can control your emotions and behaviors and helps you focus on the goals you choose to achieve. It helps you grow as a human, change what you want to change, and life in the way you decide!

According to Sonia Lobomersky, a researcher at the University of California, unhappy people spend hours comparing themselves to other people on the scale of happiness. The cheerful people did not compare themselves to anyone.

The good news is that you can use your brain to train negative thoughts that lead to frustration while increasing the types of positive thoughts.

Express happiness, and re -start your brain cells, or these young miracles known as neurons. Even if depression runs in your family, you have the ability to improve your brain functioning, set neuronal road blocks and reduce neuronal patterns associated with negative thinking. You may not be able to eliminate the genetic trend toward depression, but you can greatly reduce its effects and its regeneration.

Negative Thinking, Negative Life

Negative thinking slows down mental harmony, making it difficult to act and find solutions. Feeling frightening, which is often shown to focus on negative consequences, reduces the activity in your cerebellum, which slows down the brain's ability to take action on new information- to solve the creative problems limits your ability to practice. In addition, the fear factor affects your left temporary lob, which controls the mood, memory and continuity.

Your Frontal Lab, especially your PFC decides how important you pay attention to something and how you feel about it. That way, the more you focus on the negative, the more you will have more synapses and neurons in your mind that support your negative thinking process.

Your hippocampus provides the context of stored memories, which means that your brain that creates an emotional tone and explanation can potentially reset your brain by making strong neuronal paths and synapses. What you think and feel about a particular situation or thing can be so deep that you have to work hard to eliminate negative links and run your brain so that fear is less. Think positively, believe that dreams can come true, trusting that your efforts will be successful.

Chapter 4

Happiness Requires A Mindset Shift (How To Deal With Inner Hell)

"Pain is hell" Ajahan Sona

During the course of our life, we experience different kind of pain and suffering time to time. Pain is an important part of human life, those who run away from it or curse it increase their own pain, and if "pain is hell", then no matter where you live, it is impossible to get rid of this hell because neuroscience says our brains have a system in place to balance pain and pleasure, and when you avoid pain and spend more time on the pleasure side, it tends to increase rather than decrease. Yuval Noah says that changing places does not change the mind. Therefore pain was and is, and will remain an inherent part of your being.

There is a very strange but interesting thing about human suffering that is how our pain is determined more by how our "mind" perceives this pain than by the circumstances around us. The philosophy of

Buddhism and Stoicism believe that you taste hell in this world and that hell is within you. Right mindset is required to walk on the right path. By looking at the reality of life and surrounding and accepting it, to understand that if we want to, we can control our inner pain to some extent by controlling our brain, because according to the Buddha, it is the our mind that creates experiences, gives them meaning and leads them to happy and unhappy state.

Just as beauty is in the eye of the beholder, the attitude and perception towards pain also depends on the human mind. Situations or habits that you may find strange, boring or heartbreaking, some people find comfort or enjoyment in these situations.

Humans are extremely adaptable and set their happiness levels according to the circumstances, so it is not possible for your mind to always be in suffering. However, your mind finds happiness according to its strength and circumstances, so it is possible to maintain inner peace even in bad situations (if your brain is under your control). By using resources, one can reduce his suffering to some extent. A brain that is in confusion, fear and anxiety feels the pain more intensely.

Philosopher Albert Camus says that Sisyphus, the character of Greek mythology, who was punished for eternity by dragging a large stone up the mountain, according to Albert, the reality of our life is also like this stone. We are also Sisyphus, but Albert says that...

"Why don't we imagine that Sisyphus is dragging this stone "smiling" and very "happy"? We must imagine Sisyphus "happy and smiling" Albert Camus

Think that in this hell where there are problems everywhere and it is not possible to run away from these problems, we are stuck very badly.... So why not smile like Albert Camus's Sisyphus. Why not laugh out loud at your situation? Why not dodge the "pain"? Why not learn from the Stoic philosopher Epictetus, who even called his last day a "good day" while dying of a painful illness.

You may settle in any part of the world but remember that your inner hell i.e. that "pain" will never leave you, it will always be with you, and the same mind can keep this hell in balance.

Siddhartha Gautama, who was a lavish prince and was tired of partying day and night, one day left the palace and went on a journey to do his dopamine detox. Many people say that the Buddha was an ancient quantum physicist as well as a psychologist, who discovered that it is "attachment" that does not heal your emotional wounds. Two types of emotional attachment were mentioned by the Buddha:

1- Craving

2- Aversion

John Bowlby's attachment theory in modern psychology in which two types of attachment are described by Bowlby:

1- Anxious attachment

2- Avoidant attachment

The words are different but they both have the same meaning.

Children who have to face some events or accidents that are difficult for the underdeveloped brain of a child to understand, and it is difficult for them to feel or understand the feelings arising from these events, and if their parents/society cannot help them understand or process these feelings, then they usually end up with attachment disorder. Such people not only become unhealthily attached to people, things, places, feelings, but in many cases are under the influence of demanding or compulsive attachments.

The question arises, what is the magical and perfect attachment that does not cause you emotional pain or heals your wounds quickly??

The Buddha calls this "Non-Attachment", and modern psychology calls it "Secure Attachment". But it's not perfect and magical.

The Buddha says that craving is normal and a sign of being human, because behind the craving are sensations. When the desired object is obtained, "pleasant sensations" are felt in the body, and when an undesirable object is encountered, "unpleasant sensations" run through the body. The whole game of pleasure pain is connected to these feelings. But the problem is that some of us become overly attached to one of these feelings. The more and unhealthy the attachment, the more emotional pain you will experience, and the more you will be a slave to those feelings.

The path that Buddha discovered was the "middle one". He advised not to suppress these feelings or to want to feel them again and again, but to observe them, because you cannot eliminate the feelings, and this observation is called Mindfulness Meditation. To practice a mindful lifestyle, mindfulness meditation, or sitting with your feelings and observing them, makes you practice living in the "present moment." When you practice observing your actions, feelings, emotions, and then you no longer need meditation, but your whole life becomes meditation.

Now the question arises that what happens by observing?

When you sit with your emotions that your mind thinks are so painful that you would probably die if you endured the pain, trust me you don't. Don't die........rather you will most likely realize what the Buddha said:

"All conditions are impermanent."

"Sabbe Sankhara Anicca" (all conditioned phenomena are impermanent) Buddha

Yes! Any feeling, any emotion, any state or form is impermanent, when you observe and when your feelings become normal over a period of time, you know that it is impermanent. . It is your brain's job to hold on to old hurts and failures, because it is not easy for you to "let go" of matters that are emotionally charged.

It was intellectual understanding, but it all comes from practice, training the brain. Your brain will always try to get attached to people, to feelings, and that's natural, it's our nature to get attached, but stay in the "now", observe your emotions and actions, and be realistic and protects you from the attachment of desire, the attachment that doubles your suffering. Psychologists also use the same mindfulness technique to treat you.

Happiness is nothing but it is just a state of brain and totally depends upon you thinking, means how we look things in different situations. We are just creators of the meanings of the outer world. It is your mindset that can be your biggest ally or your worst enemy in life. And when it comes to happiness, that mindset is up there with social support and love! This can be a deal-maker or a deal-breaker.

1. Happiness doesn't mean being happy all the time.

Happiness does not mean being happy all the time. More than anything, happiness depends on your ability to be content no matter what is happening around you. You see, ups and downs are a part of life and up does not necessarily mean being extremely happy and down does not necessarily mean descending into despair. You can experience stress, sadness, and anxiety and be okay in the midst of it all, allowing you to experience true happiness.

The hedonic approach of maximizing pleasure and minimizing pain as a byproduct may help you achieve pleasure momentarily, but it won't do you much good in the long term. If you're only seeking hedonistic pleasure, you'll be trying your best to reach the pinnacles and ultimate highs of pleasure while running away from unpleasant or painful feelings. What's more, you may also be running away from lasting, long-term happiness, incidentally.

When you stop avoiding difficult times and take it little by little, responding to challenges by choosing to learn and grow from experiences instead, you will undoubtedly experience a higher level of happiness. It may sound counterintuitive. In fact, your happiness is only as limited as your feelings, your ability to tolerate and stay well during periods of distress, when you shift your mindset to embrace this thought, prepare yourself for a deep, true joy to be found.

The extent of your happiness is only limited by your ability to tolerate and recover during periods of trouble.

2. Happiness is not a feeling; it is a skill that you can build on and get better at over time.

You may have heard of the set-point theory of happiness which suggests that people's happiness is predetermined by their genes and personality traits that are set early in life. This theory, in case you haven't heard by now, has been challenged in a big way. Rather than remaining constant, happiness levels can and do change over a person's lifetime. Happiness is more of a feeling than a skill that each of us can develop and improve over time.

3. Your current position is not your final destination.

The third shift in mindset that helps you consider whether real happiness is what you yearn for believes that your current situation is not your final destination. Very closely related to #2, within this change lies the possibility of improvement, a sense of empowerment, and a life-saving essence of hope. No matter what is happening right now and how bad or unpleasant it may be you should know that it will change. It's the nature of life - change - and it's something we can always depend on.

That's why there is never any reason to give up. Sometimes no matter how painful or hard it gets, nothing stays the same. If it feels right for you to do so now, think back to one of the more difficult times in your life... a time that just plain old sucked. Have you been in this forever? Did anything come out of it? Are you ok after going through this? The truth is that in every moment of darkness there is a ray of light, and it is that ray of light that carries the torch of our lives into the next series of moments, days, weeks and years. No matter what's going on, we can mentally invite ourselves to find that little bit of hope or optimism and hold on to it, knowing that it won't be around forever.

We must understand that everything in life - every situation and every relationship - eventually come to an end. It is important to appreciate and accept the end of an era to walk away sensibly when something reaches its inevitable conclusion. Letting go, turning the page, moving on is the source of your happy life. It doesn't matter what you call it, the important thing is that you leave the past where it belongs so that you can make the best of the life that is available to live now. This is not the end; it's just that your life is starting over in a new way. This is a point in your story where one chapter fades into another.

Chapter 5

Brain Waves And How To Achieve Alpha State of Brain

With its billions of interconnected neurons, whose interactions change from millisecond to millisecond, the human brain is an archetypal complex system.

Miguel Nicolelis

In the human brain, there are always small electric fires happenings and these fires are more in number than the stars in the sky. Our brain is made up of about 86 billion sensory cells, called neurons.

These neurons transmit messages to each other in the form of small electrical pulses. In other words, we can say that the mental activities continue to illuminate our brain in the form of these amber electric fires. Brain waves occur when several sensory cells simultaneously generate electrical pulses and send messages to other sensory cells. In short, when one group of neurons sends electrical signals to another group of neurons, we call it brain waves. are

That's because a computerized electroencephalogram (EEG), which detects and measures electrical activity in your brain, actually creates an image that looks like a wave.

There are five main types of brain waves ranging from very slow to very fast. Alpha waves fall in the middle of this series of waves. Your mind creates these waves when you are awake but not focusing on one thing.

Computerized diagrams of these waves can also be obtained through EEG tests. The research has revealed that these waves are of five types according to their intensity. Each type of wave evokes a specific state of brain. The number of waves produced in one second is called the frequency of the wave. Based on the frequency range, brain waves are divided into the following five types.

1. Delta waves:

The frequency of these waves ranges from 0.5 to 4 Hz. When we are in deep sleep, our brain produces these kinds of subtle waves.

2. Theta waves:

The frequency of these waves ranges from 4 to 8 Hz. When we are in deep sleep or in a state of wakefulness we are very calm. When we are awake and asleep, our brains are generating waves.

3. Alpha waves:

The frequency range of these waves is between 8 to 12 Hz. These waves are generated by our brain when it is entering a state of flow i.e. we are starting to work in a relaxed state. This state of mind would have been highly creative

Alpha waves are at the center of your brainwave spectrum, between 8-12 Hz. When your brain is operating at the alpha frequency, you're able to absorb new information with ease and you're significantly more creative.

4. Data waves:

The frequency of these powerful waves is 12 to 35 Hz. These waves are generated by our brain when we are in a state of full awareness. In this condition, our mind is working with complete control and taking decisions.

5. Gamma Waves:

When our brain is generating very powerful waves of frequency above 35 Hz, these waves are called gamma waves. Processing information, learning, solving problems and questions are activities that require a lot of energy. In this case, the brain produces gamma waves, which are the most powerful mental waves.

An alpha brain off-state is a preferred state of brain. It is proven to cure depression and mental stress. By generating beta and gamma waves, the brain is working under extreme stress, so the nerves cannot tolerate them for long. With the help of meditation and mental exercises we can increase the production of alpha waves. Apart from this, psychologists have compiled several tips, by following which we can incorporate alpha waves into our daily life. Can it also happen by listening to music playing in very dull and slow tones and by sitting for a while in a quiet asana of yoga or meditation? But whenever we are in this state, our brain is producing alpha waves. Alpha waves seem to be the key to having moments of calm and overcoming depression and hypertension. Researchers have developed a number of techniques that we can use to set our brains to a frequency that produces alpha waves.

How to get alpha state of mind

The alpha state of mind is a state of relaxed alertness and calmness often associated with meditation and deep relaxation. It is characterized by brainwave patterns in the range of 8-12 Hz. Achieving the alpha state can help reduce stress, enhance creativity, and promote a sense of well-being. Here are some techniques that may help you get into the alpha state of mind:

Ways to get into your alpha-waves frequency

Remember that everyone's experience may vary, and it may take time to reach the alpha state consistently. Be patient and allow yourself to explore different techniques to find what works best for you.

> ➢ Find a quiet and comfortable environment: Choose a peaceful space where you can relax without interruptions. It could be a quiet room in your home or a serene outdoor location.
> ➢ Relax your body: Sit or lie down in a comfortable position. Close your eyes and

begin to relax your body starting from your toes and gradually moving up to your head. Release any tension or tightness you may be feeling.

➢ Deep breathing: Take slow, deep breaths. Inhale deeply through your nose, hold the breath for a few seconds, and exhale slowly through your mouth. Focus your attention on your breath and let go of any distracting thoughts.

➢ Progressive muscle relaxation: Starting from your toes, consciously tense and then relax each muscle group in your body. Move up slowly, tensing and relaxing your feet, calves, thighs, abdomen, hands, arms, shoulders, neck, and face. This technique helps release physical tension and promotes relaxation.

➢ Visualize a peaceful scene: Imagine yourself in a serene and calming environment such as a beach, a forest, or a meadow. Visualize the details of the scene, including the sights, sounds, and sensations. Engage your senses to create a vivid and immersive experience.

➢ Practice mindfulness: Focus your attention on the present moment without judgment. Pay attention to your thoughts, feelings, and sensations as they arise, and gently bring your focus back whenever your mind starts to wander. Mindfulness meditation can help calm the mind and induce the alpha state.

➤ Use guided imagery or meditation: You can use audio recordings or apps that provide guided imagery or meditation exercises specifically designed to induce the alpha state. These recordings often feature soothing music, calming voiceovers, and instructions for relaxation.

➤ Practice regularly: Consistency is key. Regular practice can help you train your mind to enter the alpha state more easily over time. Set aside a dedicated time each day for your relaxation practice, even if it's just a few minutes.

➤ Deep breathing and closed-eye visualization are techniques that mindfulness meditation usually employ to boost alpha waves. Besides relaxation, alpha waves may also help boost creativity. They also act as a natural anti-depressant by promoting the release of the neurotransmitter serotonin.

➢ Remove distractions from the work area. According to one study, once your focus is off an object, it takes an average of fifteen minutes to refocus on it.

➢ Identify the most energetic part of your day. Usually these are early morning, lunch and after dinner hours. Quieting your mind for a while during these times can ensure maximum production of alpha waves, which will reduce your stress level.

➢ Listening to music based on alpha waves can also put your mind in a state of producing alpha waves. You can find hours of Alpha Music tracks by searching "Alpha Music" on Google. This soothing music without rhymes can also improve your focus.

➢ Two hundred milligrams of coffee (approx consuming one and a half standard coffee mugs) can also help in generating alpha waves. This amount of coffee helps you focus on something for a longer period of time. More than this will trigger beta and gamma waves that destroy relaxation and sedation.

➢ Consuming adequate amounts of water will also help in generating alpha waves. 75% of our brain consists of water. The brain needs an uninterrupted supply of water to perform at its best, so consume more water. Especially in hot weather, so that our mind can relax and continue to produce alpha waves.

Chapter 6

Your Happy Chemicals - The Science of Happiness

Nothing captures the biological argument better than the famous New Age slogan: "Happiness begins within." Money, social status, plastic surgery, beautiful houses, powerful positions—none of these will bring you happiness. Lasting happiness comes only from serotonin, dopamine, and oxytocin.

YUVAL NOAH HARARI

There are certain hormones in your body that rise and fall throughout the day, and regularly inform you when you feel hungry, happy, and sad.

The body has an amazing system that controls the production and release of hormones. It is a network of glands that run throughout the body, each gland making at least one hormone that is controlled by the pituitary gland in the brain. Happy chemicals are controlled by tiny brain structures that are similar in all mammals: the hippocampus, amygdala, pituitary, hypothalamus, and various other parts collectively known as the limbic system. The human limbic system is surrounded by a vast cortex. The limbic system and cortex are always working together to keep you alive. Each part has its own special function: Your cortex looks for patterns in the present that match patterns you've associated within the past.

Your limbic system releases neurochemicals that tell your body "this is good for you, go for it," and "this is bad for you, avoid it." Your body doesn't always act on these messages because your cortex can override them. If the cortex overrides a message, it generates a choice and your limbic system responds to that. So your cortex may momentarily disrupt your limbic system, but your mammal brain is the core of who you are. Your cortex directs attention and filters information, but your limbic brain sparks your actions.

Your Brain's Quest to Feel Good

The search for good feelings is nature's earliest survival quest. Animals look for food to overcome the bad feeling of hunger. They seek heat to ward off the bad feeling of cold. The happy chemicals start flowing before a mammal is eaten or warmed up because the mammal brain triggers them as soon as it sees a way to satisfy the need.

The human brain does this with the added boost of a cortex that makes a long chain of associations. We avoid hunger by eating food and we avoid cold by sitting in front of heat and fire. We anticipate bad feelings to stop them. But sad chemicals persist no matter how well you meet your needs because your existence is threatened as long as you are alive.

When a mammal forages for food there is a risk of being eaten by a predator. His risk is social conflict when he seeks a mate and it risks genetic destruction if he avoids that conflict altogether. The mammal brain doesn't stop scanning for potential threats.

When you are protected from physical threats, your brain scans for social threats. Mammals survive because the bad feeling of cortisol alerts you in time to avoid potential dangers.

Cortisol communicates the expectation of pain. It motivates you to do whatever is necessary to stop the bad feeling. When the Gazelle smells a lion, cortisol prompts it to run, even as it continues to eat.

Gazelles survive because smelling a lion feels worse than hunger. Our ancestors survived because cortisol turned their attention to one threat after another.

Tony Robbins writes very beautifully about the science of happiness and its long-lasting impact on human life:

We are born to seek pleasure and happiness and to avoid pain. We have given life not only to survive but to experience happiness, joy, and fulfillment. The happiness episode starts with our Brain's chemistry that is designed in a way to releasing chemicals in the brain that make us feel good. There are many neurotransmitters or substances released by nerve fibers that trigger our feelings of happiness.

Here we will discuss the four primary chemicals that are very much responsible for all kinds of happy emotions and are known as the happy chemicals:

- **Serotonin**

- **Dopamine**

- **Oxytocin**

• **Endorphins**

Serotonin

The Happiness Chemical

Serotonin is a very important and essential neurotransmitter that is created in the brain. It circulates in the blood and throughout the central nervous system. Some scientists also refer to serotonin as the "happiness chemical," because high serotonin levels increase feelings of Happiness, self-confidence. when you feel important or valued by those around you, your Serotonin levels increase speedily.

How to Trigger Your Serotonin

There are some effective technics and strategies to trigger serotonin levels and, if you want a happier life, do this.

1. Exercise Regularly

Exercise is a very important part of a happy life that can increase serotonin levels. Any type of exercise you can do - from yoga to cycling - can be effective in increasing serotonin levels.

2. Improve Your Diet

Diet is a factor to boost Serotonin levels which are produced from the essential amino acid known as tryptophan. Tryptophan is a must to produce Serotonin because our body doesn't produce it naturally, you must get tryptophan from your diet.

To get tryptophan you can take some foods having high levels of tryptophan include:

• Salmon

• Eggs

• Soy products like tofu and soy sauce

• Poultry like chicken and turkey

• Spinach

• Seeds and nuts such as pumpkin seeds and walnuts

3. Spend time in Sunlight

Have you heard of the term seasonal depression, which is also known as seasonal affective disorder (SAD)? It's very important to take sunlight to your happiness. You know very well that when the winter approaches, it starts getting darker much earlier in the day, which can affect your mood and make you feel sad. If you suffer from depression or seasonal affective disorder, go for a short walk outside at least one time a day for spending some time in direct sunlight that can be very helpful for Generating happiness.

"The brain produces serotonin in response to the sun and daylight," Winsberg says.

4. Take Massage

Massage therapy is also a good factor for the production of serotonin levels by an average of 28%. Massage therapies are able to reduce your cortisol level and increase serotonin levels, which send you in a calmer state where you feel better, as well as regulate your mood.

Winsberg says. "This type of safe and nurturing touch can come from a loved one, partner, or professional massage therapist,"

The low level of Serotonin causes so many mental and health problems associated with digestion, blood clotting, bone density, bowel movements, nausea, and sleep patterns. It can also affect your ability to heal wounds by clotting blood. On the other hand, too much serotonin can play a role in osteoporosis and can lower your libido.

So there is a question that, does serotonin produces happiness? The simple answer is yes - and you don't need to rely on your natural serotonin levels. Hugs with your partner, aerobic exercise, getting out in the sun, getting a massage, and even watching something that makes you happy can all increase your serotonin levels.

Dopamine

The Motivational Hormone

Dopamine is another chemical that is responsible for our happiness as well as keeps us alive. It is involved in a wide range of activities, Here we are mentioning some activities include:

• Motor Control and Cognitive Functions

• The brain's motivation and reward system

• Decision making and impulse control

• Memory and Attention

• Maternal and reproductive behavior.

This chemical is a part of the brain's reward system – it's what gives you pleasant sensations. Dopamine is considered the motivational molecule in this system, and it is released naturally when you experience food or sex, but before you consume it.

Dopamine is the happiness hormone related to addictions to drugs, alcohol, and behaviors such as gambling and sex.

Dopamine is a chemical messenger in your brain. It is essential for motivation, movement, memory, mood, sleep, and behavior regulation. Dopamine is also a center point to how the brain's reward system works. Whenever you engage in a beneficial behavior, dopamine rewards you and prompts you to repeat that behavior.

Every time we do something enjoyable, like taking a good meal, having sex, or going for a run, our brain releases a little amount of dopamine. However, engaging in indulgences such as alcohol or recreational drugs also causes dopamine to be released in the brain. This is why the chemical messenger has been closely linked to addiction.

How to Increase Your Dopamine Levels

However, there are some techniques and strategies that you can use to generate your dopamine as well.

1 Take enough sleep

Getting enough amount of sleep every night is essential to maintain our health and helps to trigger our happy chemicals like Dopamine, When we don't get enough sleep, the dopamine receptors in our body can be adversely affected.

2 Listen to some music

Music can play a vital role in Generating Dopamine. Listen to some of your favorite music and it will provide you an amazing experience that can lead to triggering Dopamine.

There is a study that took place in 2011, that results when you listen to some music you feel pleasurable, it may trigger the release of dopamine in your brain.

3 Plan a healthy diet

Eating a healthy diet has many benefits for both your body and mind and increasing your dopamine levels is just a part of it. Foods rich in tyrosine such as almonds, egg yolks, and chicken are especially good for increasing dopamine levels.

Tyrosine is an amino acid that is naturally produced by the body. Dopamine is made from this amino acid and can be found in protein-rich foods. Drinks like coffee and tea also increase your dopamine levels but keep in mind that after taking it your dopamine levels drop, this can lead to caffeine addiction.

4 Exercise

Exercising regularly has proven to be very important for your brain health. It can also help you increase your dopamine levels. Your brain releases some dopamine whenever you exercise.

Does Dopamine Make You Happy?

Dopamine is another neurotransmitter made in the brain and distributed through various pathways to affect bodily functions such as heart rate, blood vessel and kidney function, nausea, vomiting, and even pain. But does dopamine make you happy? It is perhaps most famous for its role in the science of happiness.

Your body releases dopamine as part of the reward system – after sex or a good meal, or when you reach a goal. Hence it is known as the "reward molecule". As such, it plays a role in how quickly and efficiently you work. You often see that if you achieve a purpose, your mind will be flooded with dopamine in the body making you feel happy and fulfilled. This is not only true for achieving big goals. Even when you complete a small task, your dopamine levels will rise. Dopamine makes pleasure feel invigorating and invigorating. People with low levels of dopamine may experience depression or other mood disorders and may have trouble staying on task and concentrating.

Dopamine is another important answer to which chemical makes you happy – and like serotonin, you can naturally increase its levels. Exercise again plays a role here, as well as avoiding processed foods, sugar, and caffeine. But what's the best way to keep dopamine levels high? get a good night's sleep.

Oxytocin

The Love Hormone

Oxytocin is a member of the happy hormone family that is responsible for bonding and trust. It's is also known by other names like love hormone, cuddle hormone or bonding hormone. This is particularly active during labor where it stimulates contractions. One of its important functions is to regulate stress responses and calm the nervous system.

This has been indicated in establishing human connection, generosity, and trust, while other studies suggest it may be what makes some romantic relationships work. Higher blood oxytocin levels have been linked to greater perceived love, accountability, and gratitude in couples.

oxytocin plays a vital role in human bonding. Childbirth and breastfeeding is an important factor in the bond between parent and infant.

Hugging, kissing, friendships, and sexual intimacy can all trigger oxytocin production, which can strengthen bonds between couples.

These effects have led to grouping oxytocin with other happy hormones – hormones that have a positive effect on mood and emotions.

However, it is important to understand that oxytocin does not magically change your behavior. But it can increase drastically your feelings of love, contentment, security, and trust in someone you already care about.

How to Produce Oxytocin

1. Try Yoga

Yoga is a wonderful tool to increase Oxytocin levels and is responsible for so many benefits, including:

• less production of stress

• gives relief from depression

• provides better sleep

• provides Better quality of life

2. Listen to Music

While music tastes can vary widely from person to person, most people enjoy listening to some type of music.

You probably listen to music because you enjoy it, but you may have noticed that it has other benefits, such as improving your mood, focus, and motivation. It also seems to help improve the ability to form social bonds – an effect also from oxytocin.

Research is still limited, but some small studies have shown that music can help increase oxytocin levels in your body:

A 2015 study asked four jazz singers to perform two different songs: one improvised, one composed. When the singers improvised, their oxytocin levels went up. The study authors suggest that this happened because immediate exposure demands strong social behaviors such as cooperation, trust, and communication.

According to a study done on 20 open-heart surgery patients who listened to music while in bed had higher oxytocin levels and felt more relaxed than the patients who didn't listen to music.

Oxytocin levels increased in all participants after a singing lesson, in a 2003 study of 16 singers. Study participants also reported feeling more energized and relaxed.

From this point, we can say that listening to music can improve our happiness levels.

3. Take a soft touch of massage

A 2012 study on 95 adults found that a 15-minute massage could not only help people relax, but could also increase oxytocin levels.

Research from 2015 supports and expands on this finding, noting that oxytocin levels also increase in a person who is massaged.

What does massage do for you? Well, people often complain of less pain, tension, and anxiety after a massage. Many people also notice an improved mood and greater feelings of well-being.

You don't even need to have a professional massage to see these benefits. Research shows that massage from a partner or another loved one can work as well.

4. Tell Someone How Much You Care him

Sharing your love and affection with the people who mean the most to you can help increase oxytocin levels in a few ways:

• Sharing your feelings with a loved one.

• Talking to a friend or a partner you love and hug him, squeeze his hand by holding in your hand, or kiss his neck, lip, and provide him a good touch of your warm lips that will produce an amazing sensation for him.

• Telling someone how much you appreciate him. This habit can increase feelings of happiness on both sides.

5. Spend time with friends

Strong friendships can make a big difference in your emotional state. Enjoying with friends can give you great pleasure, as well as help you feel socially supported and less alone in the world.

That's the way for oxytocin to work. The good feelings you experience around your friends can help you feel more positive about your interactions, making you want to spend more time together. Your trust and affection for them also increase when you share their company more often.

Whether you make specific plans or just enjoy hanging out, the more time you spend together, the stronger your bond will be.

6. Meditation

A daily meditation practice can help in reducing stress and anxiety, and improving your state of well-being, and help you feel more compassion for yourself and others. These influences can go a long way toward increasing your sense of connection and strengthening your relationships with others.

But you can also target oxytocin production by focusing your attention on someone you care about. known as compassion meditation, involves directing thoughts of love, compassion, and goodwill toward someone in your life and sending thoughts of peace and well-being toward them.

7. Value your conversation

Active (or empathetic) listening is a fundamental principle of strong social interactions and relationships.

Connecting and enhancing feelings of connection, trust, and empathy can sometimes be as simple as actually listening to what someone has to say. It's easy to tell someone that you care about the things that matter to them, but it shows that you really do mean it.

So, when your friend or partner wants to talk about something important, keep away yourself from anything that might distract you, make eye contact, and give them your full attention. This close contact can trigger your oxytocin level, which helps you feel more connected to each other.

8. Cooking and having meals with loved ones

There are certain Studies on chimpanzees that proved that sharing food with others is a very important tool to increase oxytocin.

It also makes sense for humans – sharing a meal is a great way to create a bond between two or more persons. Think back to your middle school or elementary days. Preparing a meal with friends or a partner has provided nourishment as well as pleasure. It's my experience that when I was in university. When friends of mine used to cook the meal, and then we ate together. It was an awesome feeling. You don't just share prepared meals; You spend time with the people you love and bond with them that can generate the Oxytocin hormone.

And don't forget, the act of eating itself can create pleasure—in fact, enough to trigger oxytocin release.

9. Have sex

Sexual intimacy – especially intercourse – is an important way to increase oxytocin levels and as it provides an amazing touch with the partner as well as it's a means of wonderful affection for your partner.

Having sex with a romantic partner can help you feel closer and more connected, and you experience it through the increase in oxytocin levels. Having sex improves your mood and makes you feel great.

The best part of sexual intercourse is that both you and your partner get the boost in oxytocin levels.

10. Hug loved one

Other forms of physical intimacy, such as hugging or kissing, can also trigger oxytocin production in your body.

Hugging, holding hands can all work. So take a few moments to have a nice, long hug with your partner, child, or even your pet.

11. Do something nice for someone

- Giving someone a gift or treating them with some kind of kindness makes them happy, which can make you feel happy too. The simple act of brightening up someone's day can lift your spirits and also foster positive emotions in you. So if you would like to live life generously. You can try:

- Offer to help a neighbor

- Giving a few extra dollars to charity

- Support your favorite cause

- Buying gift cards for a friend or family member etc.

12. Pet Dogs

If you are an animal lover then this is the best news for you!

Research shows that both dogs and humans show an increase in oxytocin levels from physical contact,

So it can be very comforting to hug your animal friend when you are upset. The oxytocin produced by your conversations helps you feel a little better.

Although this research only looked at human-dog interactions, it's pretty safe to say that petting your cat or giving your bird some head scratches would probably have a similar effect.

Oxytocin Boost occurs in response to perceived stimuli by the brain, which is carefully monitoring your environment for threats (and safety cues) using your ears, eyes, taste, touch, and smell. It is produced in contact, and even with the right kind of eye contact, but also to balance the effects of cortisol in times of stress.

In recent years, the scientific community has found that oxytocin plays a much broader role than initially prescribed, regulating the immune system, healing, and even pain perception. You won't be surprised to learn that your gut bacteria have gotten their finger on this pie as well.

Although most studies have been done in rats, it has been shown that gut microbes can stimulate oxytocin production, thus promoting wound healing and muscle health, leading some to suggest that this chemical is involved in contributing to healthy longevity.

Endorphins

The Runner's Hormone

Endorphins are hormones and neuro-signaling molecules that act as pain relievers. They block the transmission of pain signals in the central nervous system by binding to opioid receptors (the body's natural morphine).

What are endorphins?

Let's start with this word: endorphins. The name comes from two words: endogenous (meaning coming from the body) and morphine (opium pain reliever). So it makes sense that endorphins are your body's natural pain reliever. But what are they really?

Endorphins are a group of peptides that are produced by your pituitary gland and central nervous system and that act on opiate receptors in your brain. These neurotransmitters also act to increase feelings of pleasure and well-being and to reduce pain and discomfort.

Have you ever experienced a rush of endorphins? It usually occurs in response to a specific event such as eating a certain food, engaging in a form of exercise, engaging in intercourse, experiencing a stressful situation, or experiencing something physically painful.

For example, if you were jogging in the woods and sprained your ankle, you may experience a surge in endorphins that will help you stay safe out of the woods despite your injury. Or, endorphins may explain why a group of people can lift a vehicle heavier than an injured pedestrian after a traffic accident, while under normal circumstances they cannot do so.

Endorphins help keep us away from feelings of pain and leading us toward feelings of pleasure. Without the production of your endorphins, your world would probably become less colorful.

Benefits of Endorphins

Endorphins can have many positive effects in terms of your health and well-being. Imagine you are on vacation and you are bitten by a snake, yet you do not feel any pain. why? Because there is a huge surge of Endorphins in your brain at that moment which results in the protective effect of a surge of endorphins, helping you cope with the stress of the situation.

There are many benefits of endorphins.

• Less depression

• less worry

• Better self-esteem

• An increased immune response

• Less Pain

As you can see, endorphins have many benefits. In fact, getting regular exercise such as exercising for 45 minutes three times per week at moderate intensity may be a good first option for those living with mild depression.

Now the question arises that how to trigger you're Endorphins?

What can you do to increase your natural endorphins? Contrary to what you might think, you don't need to run a marathon or do anything outrageous to boost your endorphins to achieve a runner's height.

While it's true that high-intensity workouts will produce more endorphins than low-intensity workouts, there are many different ways you can boost your endorphins without crossing the finish line after 26.2 miles.

Below is a list of simple options that you can start with right away.

1. Have a Dark Chocolate

Do you like chocolate? If yes, then it's a good chance for you and like. You have good luck. Eating just one piece of dark chocolate can help boost your endorphins.

2. Have Sex

When you have intercourse, your body also releases endorphins. Not only are you engaging in physical exercise, but you are also forming a social bond with another person.

3. Dance

If you don't feel like running or doing a regular workout, simply dancing in your house can increase your endorphins as well.

4. Get in a Good Laugh

Laughter can also stimulate your endorphins, so make sure to try to have a good laugh every day. Watch TV shows full of comedy and humor, or spend time with people who make you laugh.

5. Eat Spicy Food

Did you know that eating spicy foods can trigger your endorphins? It's a good excuse to go to an Indian restaurant or pick up a new spicy item from the menu the next time you go out to eat.

6. Take massage

Massage can also help increase your endorphins. It's not even a professional massage; You can ask your partner to massage you, sit down in a massage chair, or use a portable massager to relax tense muscles.

7. Do Volunteer Work

When you volunteer, you are not only doing good to others but also increasing your endorphins. This is another easy way to improve your feelings of well-being.

8. Spend time with friends

Friends are like jewels and spending time with them can help increase your endorphin levels and create a sense of happiness for you.

Endorphins vs Dopamine

What is the difference between endorphins and dopamine in your brain? While endorphins are neurotransmitters that help you deal with pain and stress, dopamine is a mood-boosting neurotransmitter that is released once you reach your goal.

In this way, dopamine is involved in reward circuits in your brain and helps motivate you toward tasks (conversely, low dopamine will also de-motivate). Higher endorphins can actually lead to higher dopamine production; In this way, endorphins and dopamine are not mutually exclusive but are linked in the system that promotes action toward rewards and results in good feelings.

In other words, you may feel motivated to run a marathon because of your dopamine reward system, which is further reinforced by the endorphins released during the actual act of participating in the race. In this way, endorphins are fast-acting "feelings", while dopamine is the long-acting afterglow.

Endorphins and dopamine are often confused because each is a chemical that makes you happy in the broadest sense of the word. However, they are related in some ways, because when endorphins bind to receptors in the central nervous system, dopamine (the hormone of happiness) is released.

Still, happy endorphins rose to fame not because they block pain signals, but because they induce euphoria. That's right, the ubiquitous "runner's high" is caused by a huge rush of endorphins. In addition, the powerful combination of endorphins and dopamine explains why people tend to "get hooked" when they run.

Endorphins make you happy after exercise.

Cortisol

The Enemy of Happiness

Cortisol is a hormone produced by the body's adrenal glands. In moderate amounts, it reduces inflammation in the body and regulates blood pressure, blood sugar, and sleep. It is also the body's main stress hormone and is most well-known for inciting the "fight-or-flight" response. When you are in a constant state of stress, cortisol tends to be elevated. Not only does this state reduce our happiness, but it also negatively affects memory and attention, can lead to weight gain, and can have serious effects on our major organs and immune systems.

How Does Cortisol Work?

Cortisol is your body's emergency transmission system, when it feels existential threat from various dangerous events. This creates the feeling that humans call "pain". Pain deserves your attention. It feels bad because it works - it focuses your attention on what is needed to stop it.

The brain tries to avoid pain by storing the details of the experience so that you know what to look for in the future. When you see things related to past pain, your cortisol starts flowing so that you can take timely action to avoid future pain. A large brain can generate multiple associations, so it can anticipate many possible sources of pain. When cortisol increases, we call it "fear," but when cortisol decreases, we call it "anxiety" or "stress." These bad feelings tell you that pain will come if you don't act fast. Your reptilian brain can't explain why it released cortisol. Lightning was flowing through a path. When you understand how this happens, you can more easily distinguish between internal alarms and external threats. You might think that if the world was in a better state you would be free of cortisol. But your brain sees every disappointment as a threat, and this response has value. It alerts you in time to prevent further failures and disappointments. For example, if you've walked miles to get to the water and suddenly you realize that you're on the wrong track, a wave of bad feelings keeps you from walking furthermore toward the wrong path. You can't predict accurately all the time, so your cortisol will always have to work. By understanding the cortisol chemistry you can create peace in your brain that leads to an amazing world of Happiness as well as you can discover the world filled with happiness and joy around you.

Chapter 7

Common Reasons of Your Unhappy State

We create our own unhappiness. The purpose of suffering is to help us understand we are the ones who cause it.

Willie Nelson

Why a man does experiences happiness while the other one feels unhappiness? One's life is full of happiness, while the second one experiences miseries, problems, and unhappiness?

This is a basic phenomenon of the world through which many pass and experience it in day and nightlife. The entire problems of life return to understand the real mental process of the human brain, and how we think and design our life.

First of all, we must know the reasons why we are unhappy.

Here are 7 basic reasons for Unhappiness:

1. Not Doing the Things You Love Most

Remember when you were young, carefree, and were ready to do whatever you like to do so.

If you wanted to enjoy a game, you did. If you wanted to dance, you used to dance. And as the result, you felt happy after doing so. You didn't have to worry about client calls, angry boss. Now you're all grown up, and well, life's done.

But despite the hectic, energy-packed, and sometimes mundane nature of everyday adult life, it's still necessary to find time for your hobbies.

It's grown-up that you may not have the luxury of paying to play and dance. But, you should find time to play and dance to have fun and revel in the joy of it all. It will put a jolt of positive energy into your life!

2. Competition with Others

Contrary to many people's beliefs, life is not really a competition. It's a marathon against you and competition with the person you were yesterday. No one else is following your track.

When we treat life like a race to the top, happiness will remain elusive. There will always be someone wiser, smarter, richer, and sweeter. So what? Are you going to be sad because someone else seems to be better? They may be better than you in one area, but this is not true in every area. It is your responsibility to recognize, nurture your unique gifts and strengths.

3. Less self-care

Don't get so busy neglecting your body and mind. A good diet and exercise routine will not only improve your overall health, but it will also help you look and feel good!

Also, take care of your mind. This is your most important asset with unlimited capabilities and potential.

Invest in your brain and let it marvel with your brand. Read books, learn new habits and constantly add value to your mind. Not only will this increase your perception and understanding, but you will also feel happier and more confident.

4. Not Spending Time with Happy People

It is your friendships and connectedness with the people that affect your emotional state and feeling of being Happier.

Studies show that people who spent time with happy people were more likely to be happy and had a sense of betterment.

So, spend time with positive, inspiring people and enjoy their happiness. Don't be with those who are living in a negative world as if the world's problems are on their shoulders.

5. *Not Expressing Gratitude*

Are you finding it difficult to express gratitude because your life is not going according to plan? Or you have gone through some terrible experience in the past that you will be angry and bitter. Well, don't be. There is still much to be thankful for.

You have your family, who loves and values you, despite occasional squabbles. your friends, some of whom will walk through walls for you; And your work, which may not be perfect, but continues to wake you up in the morning. Heck, you even have your enemies, who through their actions have taught you how to make you stronger and wiser in the face of hatred as well. And then you are! You have made it so distant, alive, and strong. And the fact that you are reading this means that you have not given up on the growth potential. Despite challenges, disappointments, sorrows, countless inaccuracies, you are better than you were yesterday and you have indeed made progress. Be grateful for the fact that you survived, because not everyone has.

6. Living in The Past

Everyone has had some difficult and painful past experiences, but great achievers believe that the past does not define them. They draw valuable insights from these experiences and use them as inspiration for greater success.

By holding onto grudges, you stir up negative emotions—regret, resentment, and bitterness—and plunge yourself into more misery. As a result, your productivity and work may be affected. Let go! Keep moving towards greater levels of happiness, productivity and success.

7. You Don't Want To Get Help

Are the reasons for your unhappiness out of your control? Perhaps you are struggling with habits or addictions? Get help for your sake, and for the countless others who will benefit from your happiness, productivity, and success!

Your inner circle may be more valuable than you think in this regard. Just talking to a family member, friend, or close relative can be all the help you need.

For long-term and deeper problems, it will be necessary to see a professional. By going whole-heartedly for counseling, therapy, or even rehabilitation, you will begin the necessary process of taking back control of your life and happiness.

Chapter 8

7 Proven Habits To Achieve Unconditional Happiness

The art of being happy lies in the power of extracting happiness from common things.

Henry Ward Beecher

There are a few ways you can try to find unconditional happiness. But here, we will throw light on 7 highly recommended tools by scientists and psychologists to achieve unconditional and long-lasting happiness.

1. Achieve Your Goals

Achieving goals that you are intrinsically motivated to pursue, especially those focused on personal development and community can help promote happiness. Research suggests that pursuing these types of intrinsically motivated goals can lead to greater happiness than pursuing extrinsic goals, such as achieving wealth or status.

2 Understand the Power of Now

Studies have shown that people tend to earn more - they become so focused on hoarding things that they lose track of actually enjoying what they are doing. So, instead of falling into the trap of accumulating thoughtlessly to the detriment of your happiness, focus on practicing gratitude for what you have and enjoying the process.

3. Kill Your Negative Thoughts

When you find yourself stuck in a pessimistic outlook or experience negativity, look for ways you can change your thoughts to a more positive one.

People have a natural negativity bias, or a tendency to focus more on bad things than on good things. It can have an impact on everything from how you make decisions to how you form impressions of other people. Discounting the positive – a cognitive distortion where people focus on the negative and ignore the positive – can also contribute to negative thoughts.

Reshaping these negative thoughts is not about ignoring the bad. Instead, it means trying to take a more balanced, realistic look at events. It allows you to notice patterns in your thinking and then challenge negative thoughts.

4. Positive emotions increase resilience.

Resilience helps people better manage stress and bounce back better when faced with setbacks. For example, one study found that happy people had lower levels of the stress hormone cortisol, and these benefits persisted over time.

5. Get Regular Exercise

Exercise is good for both your body and mind. Physical activity has been linked to a range of physical and psychological benefits, including improved mood. Several studies have shown that regular exercise can play a role in relieving symptoms of depression, but evidence also suggests that it can also help make people happier.

In an analysis of previous research on the association between physical activity and happiness, researchers found a consistently positive relationship between them.

Even a little exercise boosted happiness—happiness compared to people who were physically active for at least 10 minutes a day or who worked out only once a week.

6. Show Gratitude

In one study, participants were asked to engage in a writing exercise for 10 to 20 minutes before bedtime each night. Some were instructed to write about daily troubles, some about neutral events, and some about things they were grateful for. The results found that those who wrote about gratitude experienced increased positive feelings, increased subjective happiness, and improved life satisfaction.

As the study authors suggest, keeping a gratitude list is a relatively easy, economical, simple, and enjoyable way to boost your mood. Try writing down a few minutes each night or thinking about the things in your life that you are grateful for.

7. Find a Purpose Driven Life

Last but not least among the above-mentioned factors to have a happy life, purpose-driven life is a wonderful gift.

Research has found that people who feel they have a purpose have better well-being and feel more fulfilled. A sense of purpose involves seeing your life as having goals, direction, and meaning. It can help improve happiness by promoting healthy behaviors.

There are things you can do to help find a sense of purpose including:

• Explore your interests and passions

• Engage in charitable work to correct injustice

• Discover new things you might want to know more about

This sense of purpose is influenced by a variety of factors, but it is also something you can develop. It involves finding a goal that you care about deeply that will motivate you to engage in productive, positive actions to work toward that goal.

It is very important to consider how you personally define happiness. Happiness is a broad term that means different things to different people. It is very important to think about what happiness really means to you and then work on the little things that will help you be happy. It can make these goals more manageable and less overwhelming and focus on building and cultivating life and relationships. Which bring fulfillment and satisfaction to your life.

Tony Robbins says, *"Progress equals happiness."*

Conclusion

Dear reader,

Now, I am sure that you are equipped with all the understanding about how to trigger your Brain Power and unleash your Brain's Full Potential to achieve unconditional Happiness using happy chemicals generated by a paradigm shift in the thinking process. You are well aware of many creative techniques and strategies that can generate happiness in all spheres of your life.

I wrote this book in a manner that you could use and implement the techniques and strategies while reading the book.

Let me explain here. Though I do write my works specifically to add value to the lives of my readers (it's you!), but I always have some personal motive in my mind to get exposed to valuable insights while doing research so that I can get benefitted by implementing them in my life.

Therefore, I invite you to be a part of this journey with me to practice what we just learned in the book and deepen our experience of life by experimenting with multiple techniques in order to rewire our brain to achieve amazing secrets of happiness, joy, and fulfillment.

As we all know, repetition is the mother of learning. So let's keep exposing our minds to the resourceful information on a regular basis, and let the compound effect work to our advantage in developing a creative mind and lead a life of joy, happiness, and success. I wish you nothing but loads of success by generating and implementing great ideas in all your endeavors.

Thank you!

Abuzar Khan

THANK YOU!

BEFORE YOU GO, I WOULD like to say thank you for purchasing and reading my book.

There are a large number of other books on this subject, but you picked it amongst them. And you took a chance and checked out this one.

So, big thanks for downloading this book and reading it all the way to the end.

Now I'd like to ask for a small favor. Could you please spend a minute or two with me and leave a review for this book on your favorite book store?

Because

Reviews are Gold to the Authors!

Your feedback will help me continue to write the kind of kindle books that help you get the best results.

Thank you again!

DISCLAMER

While we have made all attempts to verify the information provided in this book, the author does not assume any responsibility for errors, omissions, or contrary interpretations of the subject matter herein.

The views expressed in the book are those of the author alone, and should not be taken as expert instruction or commands. The reader is responsible for his or her own actions.

The author makes no representations or warranties with respect to the accuracy or completeness of the contents of this work and specifically disclaims all warranties, including without limitation warranties of fitness for a particular purpose. No warranty may be created or extended by sales or promotional materials. The advice and recipes contained herein may not be suitable for everyone. This work is sold with the understanding that the author is not engaged in rendering medical, legal, or other professional advice or services. If professional assistance is required, the services of a competent professional person should be sought. The author shall not be liable for damages arising here from. The fact that an individual, organization or website is referred to in this work as a citation and/or potential source of further information does not mean that the author endorses the information the individual, organization to the website may provide or recommendations they/it may make. Further, readers should be aware that Internet Websites listed in this work might have changed or disappeared between when this work was written and when it is read. Adherence to all applicable laws and regulations, including international, federal, state, and local governing professional licensing, business practices, advertising, and all other aspects of doing business in any jurisdiction in the world is the sole responsibility of the purchaser or reader.

Other Books by Author

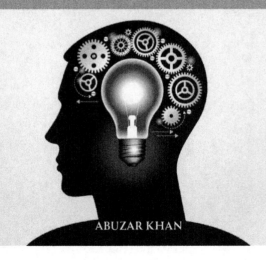

CONTROL YOUR
MIND
UNLOCK YOUR
DESTINY

Master Your Mind. Discover Your Inner
Hero. Be Highly Productive And Live The
Life You Want

ABUZAR KHAN

THE POWER OF READING

TODAY A READER, TOMORROW A LEADER

ABUZAR KHAN

A HAPPIER
BRAIN

Switch On Your Brain. Boost Your Serotonin,
Dopamine, Oxytocin, & Endorphin Levels. Unlock
Your Happier, Healthier and More Abundant Life

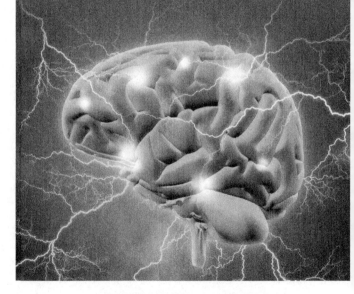

ABUZAR KHAN

Sources

(1) HABITS OF A HAPPY BRAIN: Retrain Your Brain to Boost Your Serotonin, Dopamine, Oxytocin, & Endorphin Levels. LORETTA GRAZIANO BREUNING, PHD

(2) The Happy Brain: The Science of Where Happiness Comes From, and Why. DEAN Burnett

(3) THINK OUT OF THE BOX: Generate Ideas on Demand, Improve Problem Solving, Make Better Decisions, and Start Thinking Your Way to the Top. Som Bathla

(4) THE HAPPINESS HACK:How to Take Charge of Your Brain and Program More Happiness into Your Life. Ellen Petry Leanse

(5) Rewire Your Brain: Think Your Way to a Better Life. John B. Arden, Ph.D.

(6) POWER UP YOUR BRAIN: The Neuroscience of Enlightenment, DAVID, PERLMUTTER, M.D., F.A.C.N. ALBERTO VILLOLDO, PH.D.

Websites

https://www.verywellmind.com/what-is-happiness-4869755

https://mayfieldclinic.com/pe-anatbrain.htm

https://www.insider.com/how-to-increase-serotonin

https://www.healthline.com/health/happy-hormone

Printed in Great Britain
by Amazon

37695629R00059